CHILD OF SAND AND WATER

CHILD OF SAND AND WATER

BY DIANE D. KING

Mountain Air Books

Mountain Air Books
Scott Krause
1045 University Ave., Ste #9
Rochester, NY 14607
585-442-9468

ISBN: 978-0-615-41620-5

Acknowledgements:

STEVE BALDWIN
IRMA BAUMAN
KATHY CLEARY
JERRY AND ANNA MARIA DELUCCIO
CHERYL DICKERSON
RICHMOND FUTCH
MAUREEN GATES
JENNIFER HART
BIRNELLA HEGANOVIC
LEE KING
CHRISTIAN KOLUPSKI
MICHAL MCKENZIE
JANET NORTHRUP
LORETTA PETRALIS
SUSAN REINDEL
SARAH ROBINSON
ELLEN RUSLING
CAROL SAMUEL
LISA SCHWARZBAUM
CAROL SNOOK
DEBRA VANWERT
LYNNE YOUNG
LISA SMITH YOUNGDAHL
PAT YOUNGDAHL

In 1985, with tears in his eyes, Salva Dut, age 11, left his family. In Salva's words, "We had a beautiful nomadic life. I took care of our calves. My brother shepherded cows, goats and sheep. My father worked in the fields. One sister helped my mother at home by gathering the firewood and pounding grain into flour. My other sister traveled eight hours each day collecting water." But the Sudan was in the middle of a civil war.

Salva fled from his home, and a couple of years later, driven by similar fears, so did another inspirational young man, Sebastian Maroundit. Separately, but with dreams to help heal their homeland in the future, they crossed the Sahara Akoba desert. They were escaping rebels from the north who were abducting and killing young boys in southern Sudan. Five thousand of the boys died of thirst and starvation. About 12,000 made it to safety. These young men became known as **The Lost Boys**. They were protected and educated at United Nations refugee camps in Ethiopia and Kenya. Eventually sponsors throughout the world offered some of them opportunities to emigrate, and in so doing, extended the promise of education and a new life.

Arriving a few years apart, Salva and Sebastian were brought to America by Catholic Relief Services, the coordinating organization in the United States. Sponsors were located for each of them in Rochester, New York at St. Paul's Episcopal Church and Downtown United Presbyterian Church. They quickly found work and began to attend college, but never lost sight of their goals to bring water and schools to the parched villages of southern Sudan. In 2003, the war having abated, Salva established the Not-For-Profit, Water For Sudan or WFS. Sebastian's Building Minds in Sudan, BMIS, followed a few years later. As this book goes to print, Water for Sudan has installed over 180 wells, opening the door for the construction of BMIS schools, vastly improved health, and commercial growth.

On July 9, 2011 southern Sudan officially became the independent nation of South Sudan.

More information about this story and the purchase of books can be found at:
www.waterforsouthsudan.org   www.buildingmindsinsouthsudan.org

The following is a novelized version of Salva's and Sebastian's journeys which has been embellished by accounts of other Lost Boys living in the Rochester area. It contains spirit raising ditties and chants that sprang purely from the author's imagination in an attempt to inject hope into the darkest parts of the story. These elements are intended for the target audience, children in the primary grades, in order to "cast a softer light" on the harsh experience of The Lost Boys, rather than to "make light" of it.

A few Swahili words have been added to enrich the text. Although it is only an occasional lingua franca of South Sudan, Swahili was chosen for its universality in East Africa and its comforting cadence.

Boma: Village   Asante sana: Thank You   Lala salama: Good Night

The downbeat for the chant occurs on the bolded words: "My **hands** start to **wiggle** and my **feet** start to **jiggle** and I **dance**… **dance**…**dance** like a **squiggle**."

A special "thank you" to Salva Dut, Sebastian Maroundit, and other Lost Boys, Solomon Anyoun, and Peter Kuch, who shared their painful stories with grace and wisdom, to those who served as my able junior editors: Mrs. Reindel's 2007-08 2nd grade class at Brooks Hill School, Fairport, NY and Mrs. Hart's 2008-09 2nd grade class at Rochester City School #28, the hard working Boards of Water for South Sudan, Building Minds in South Sudan and Hope of South Sudan, as well as the many friends and family members who spared none of my pride in their scrutiny of my work.

MAP OF AFRICA

The Lost Boys first escaped from the Sudan to Ethiopia, but unstable conditions in Ethiopia caused them to flee again to Kenya.

Something made Salva shiver on this hot day. His mother was coming in early from the fields. His goat was butting him in the leg.

"Salva," his mother said, "give me your hand. We can walk together to greet your sister. She will be coming soon with water for the village and will be very tired. The goat can stay here. You have taken good care of her today."

Suddenly Salva's mother was crying. She hugged him and said, "While we wait for your sister I must tell you something sad. Papa heard that rebels are coming from the north. They are taking all boys away from our villages (bomas). Your uncle will help you, and the other boys from our boma, escape to Ethiopia where you will be safe until the trouble is over.

The rest of the family will run in a different direction. You must be big and brave. Remember, always, how much we love you."

"How long will I be away from my home?" Salva moaned. His mother hung her head and said, "Maybe a very, very long time." In all of his eleven years he had never been so frightened. He could not imagine living without his family. But, from the sound in his mother's voice he knew he must leave right away.

"We will think about you and love you every day," his mother reminded him again.

Salva and thousands of boys of all ages ran from their enemies in southern Sudan. They walked hundreds of miles on their own. In the desert they had almost no food or water. They ate roots and grasses and hunted animals. Their journey was scary and difficult.

Throughout the world they became known as
"The Lost Boys."

"We will keep from getting too sad by singing," said Salva. He led them in a marching song.

"One day we will see our homes again. Water and food will be plenty then."

A small boy used two sticks to beat the rhythm. They had new energy and could be on their way once more.

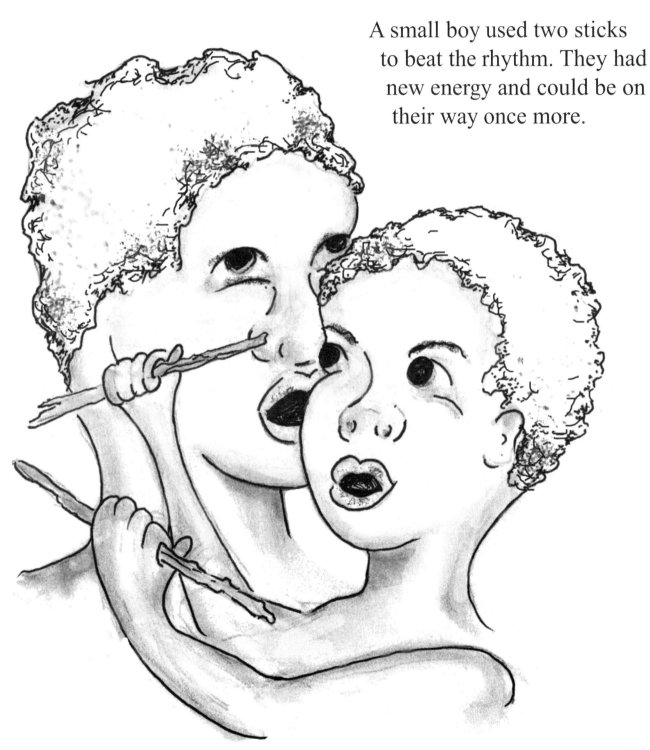

Every night Salva looked at the stars. They made him miss his family. His heart hurt. He remembered that his sister walked eight hours every day to fetch water. He said aloud to the stars, "I promise I will find water for my boma if one day I can go home."

One night a strange thing happened while he gazed at the stars. He was lying very still. Slowly, his mind connected the stars like making a picture out of dots. It looked a bit like his sister.

Then his feet tingled and shook. A new song came into his head.

♪ "My **hands** start to **wiggle**, and my **feet** start to **jiggle**, and I **dance**...**dance**...**dance** like a **squiggle**." ♪

As he hopped around, the pain in his heart lifted. His song made him think there was hope.

And suddenly, with the other Lost Boys beside him, he was dancing his way to Kenya.
"Good night, Lala salama," he whispered to his sister in the sky.

In Kenya, Kaukuma became the boys safe new home.
"This is only a refugee camp, not our boma," Salva said to his
friend. "But we are clean. We have food. Best of all, we go to
school."

He gave thanks and hugged his books.

Salva wanted to learn many things. He practiced his English with anyone who would listen.

"I...am...Salva." He said each word carefully.

"Who...are...you?"

"Now I have chances I never had before," he thought.
"I will work hard. I will be able to help my country when the fighting is over. Maybe I will even find my family."
He thought of them everyday.

ABCD...EFG..

Years passed...

Sponsors in America and Europe helped the Lost Boys find new homes.

Salva waited his turn. "Here is my name! I am going to the United States!"

"Where is the map?!"

JOHN: FRANCE

SEBASTIAN: U.S.A

SALVA: U.S.A.

Salva had never seen a plane before. As the plane took off, he wondered what else would be new in America. "Will I eat mangos and bananas? Will I ever see a giraffe again? Will I ever know whether my parents are alive? Where are my sisters and brothers?" Now he was really alone. Many friends were left behind.

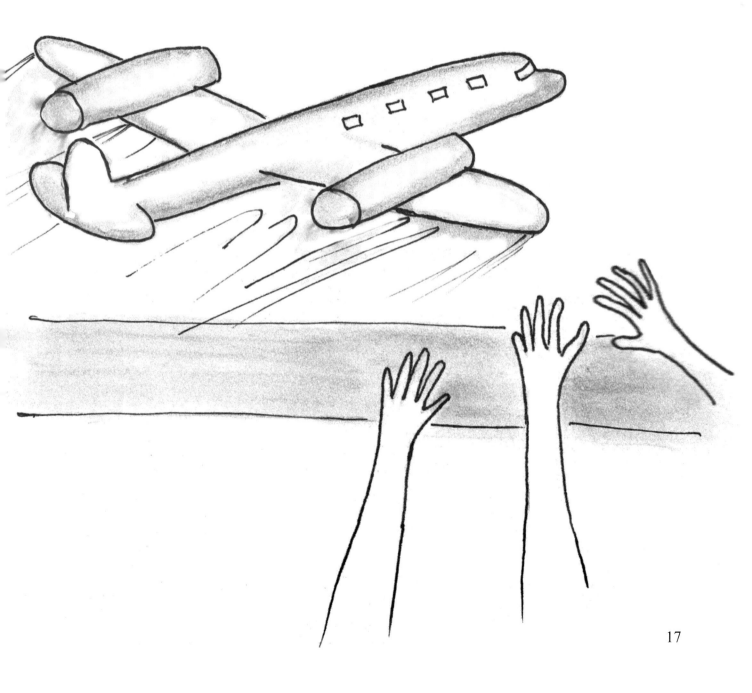

His new home was full of surprises. A church sponsored him. He was going to live in an apartment with other Lost Boys. Before they could live alone, good people from the church showed them how to cook on a stove. Salva learned to use a washing machine at the Laundromat. The washer rocked back and forth. While he watched it he felt a tingling. Suddenly he remembered something from long ago, his song of hope.

"My **hands** start to **wiggle**, and my **feet** start to **jiggle**, and I **dance...dance...dance** like a **squiggle**."

"At least one of my dreams came true," he thought. "Finally I have a chance for a good future."

Salva worked hard. He had three jobs. He got his high school diploma and then went to college. He was happy and proud. On graduation day he had to hide his hand under his gown. The joy he felt made him think ...

"My **hands** start to **wiggle** ..."

Then, a new Lost Boy arrived whose name was Sebastian. Sebastian hoped that someday, when he too graduated, he could build schools in the southern Sudan. He admired Salva.

They both dreamed for the children left behind, and talked about helping them together in the future.

Salva now had the skills to get a good job. He thanked his friends and adopted families for all their help.

He truly had a loving home in the United States. But, like Sebastian, his heart was in southern Sudan where people were sick and starving.

His friends gave him a graduation party. Then they said, as if they were reading his mind, "It's OK Salva. We know you want to follow your dream. Go to southern Sudan. The fighting is over. We will help you to help them get water."

Salva studied about water. He found out that under the ground in southern Sudan there is a huge lake called an aquifer. "How can I get the water out," he thought.

He found an East African company that drills wells. Each well cost $8,000 to drill. Churches, synagogues, schools and individuals raised money for Salva's wells. Soon money grew in the bank. All over America people began to help.

Finally he had enough money to build four wells.

He packed his suitcase for the journey home. As he left for the airport, many people were there to see him off.

Deep in his heart he had another reason to be very happy. He had good news about some of his family. They would meet again when he arrived. For so many years he had hoped. Now, more dreams were coming true.

After the plane landed he was taken to see his father. They cried and held each other. His mother and sister had not been seen in many years. Then Salva noticed that his father was sick. The disease had come from polluted water.

He knew once again that he could do something that would help save the lives of many people. He would bring clean water to the bomas of his homeland.

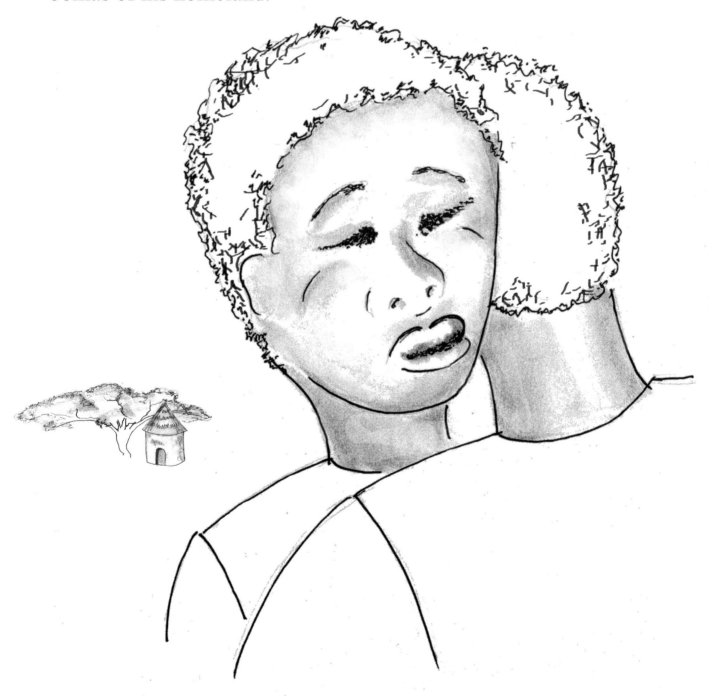

When Salva arrived in the first village everyone was excited and ready to help. Each person, young and old, could feel the change and wanted to take part in the work. The drill dug a deep hole for the long pipe that would go down to the aquifer. Villagers cleared away rocks and dirt. They knew they were building a community. All would share in the good future to come.

Finally, the first well was finished. Everyone was happy. Children cheered. No longer would they walk eight hours a day with heavy water jugs on their heads. The youngest child was picked to be the first person to drink from the pump.

Looking from one child to another, Salva said, "This was my dream. Now you can spend your time learning."

The number of wells is growing and growing. Now there are many villages where children are not carrying water all day. They sit under trees to learn, and wait patiently for schools to be built. These are known as "Under the Tree Schools." Back in America Sebastian is raising money to build real school buildings.

Now, between the bomas near the first well, there stands a building with classrooms. And as the boys and girls pass the well on their way to school they feel their ...

♪ " ... **hands** start to **wiggle**, and their **feet** ..." ♪

Surrounding each well is a circle of concrete. The names of the people or groups who gave money for the well are written in the concrete for all to see.

On July 9, 2011 southern Sudan became the independent nation of South Sudan.

Every day Salva and Sebastian give thanks (asante sana). Asante sana for being alive.

Asante sana for the new nation.
Asante sana for their educations.

Asante sana for being able to bring water and schools to South Sudan so children can be healthy and have the opportunity to learn.

Asante sana for the many people who are raising money to give the gifts of life and hope.

Here are a few of the wild animals you might find in Africa.

Antelope

Cheetah

Elephant

Gazelle

Giraffe

Photo: Steve Baldwin

SEBASTIAN MAROUNDIT
Building Minds in South Sudan (BMISS)
www.buildingmindsinsouthsudan.org

SALVA DUT
Water for South Sudan (WFSS)
www.waterforsouthsudan.org

About the Author

As co-founder of Building Minds in South Sudan Diane King continues to mentor Lost Boys in the upstate NY community. She is an active member of Journeys of Inspiration, an outdoor adventure/fund raising cancer survivor group focused on raising money for disadvantaged children in Africa, as well as for cancer. She is a retired high school counselor, ex-Peace Corps Volunteer in India, devoted wife of Sam, mother to Amy and Baird, and surrogate mother to Maciek, Ewa, Agnieszka and Nico.

During high school, while participating in a relief work project, Diane hiked into the raw humanity of the Appalachian heartland, and has never stopped wandering, wondering when, and how, world suffering will end, and we will be at peace with one another.